Richard
Branson
In His Own Words

Richard
Branson
In His Own Words

EDITED BY
Danielle McLimore

A B2 BOOK

AGATE

CHICAGO

Printed in the United States of America

ISBN 13: 978-1-57284-291-5
ISBN 10: 1-57284-291-1

10 9 8 7 6 5 4 3 2 1   20 21 22 23 24 25

The Library of Congress has cataloged a previous edition of this book as follows:

Branson, Richard.
  Virgin rebel : Richard Branson in his own words / edited by Danielle McLimore.
    pages cm. -- (In their own words)
  Summary: "A collection of direct quotes from Richard Branson on topics related to business, entrepreneurship, the Virgin Group, philanthropy, and life"--Provided by publisher"-- Provided by publisher.
  Includes bibliographical references and index.
  ISBN 978-1-932841-78-7 (pbk.) -- ISBN 1-932841-78-4 (paperback) -- ISBN 978-1-57284-725-5 (ebook)
  1. Branson, Richard--Quotations. 2. Businesspeople--Great Britain--Quotations. 3. Entrepreneurship--Quotations, maxims, etc. 4. Management--Quotations, maxims, etc. I. McLimore, Danielle. II. Title.
  HC252.5.B73A25 2013
  082--dc23
                         2013016978

Whatever we want to be, whatever we want to do, we can do it. Go ahead, take that first step—just do it. The best of luck to you, and have fun along the way.

—RICHARD BRANSON

Contents

Introduction

"**D**o what you love, and the money will follow"—no person better exemplifies this adage than multibillionaire Sir Richard Branson, who has earned his fortune simply by pursuing his personal interests. His seamless transitions from journalist to record executive to space-travel pioneer have all begun with a natural curiosity and passion, coupled with a well-honed instinct for turning anything into a business.

In 1968, at the age of 16, Branson left school to begin his first entrepreneurial venture, a magazine called *Student*. In 1970, he moved into music with a mail-order record business, and then opened his first chain of record stores, Virgin Records, just two years later. From there, he grew the Virgin brand, and became a recognizable figure worldwide. As you look through Virgin Group's widely varied list of companies (p. 151), you'll be struck by the diversity of businesses. It would seem that they all began with Branson, probably in the bath (he speaks frequently about taking baths), just pondering what he likes to do and how he can make money doing it. Virgin Galactic is a perfect example: Branson wanted to travel to space, and figured he wasn't the only one. Rather than fund the research for consumer space travel entirely out of his own pocket, he created Virgin Galactic; and now, for $250,000, anyone can purchase a trip into suborbital space (whenever the technology is ready).

Branson also knows when to cut his losses—and that doing so is just as important as knowing how and when to start a company. When a business or product isn't doing well, rather than hang on in the hopes of a turnaround, he will often just pack it in and move on. Virgin Pulse (a line of electronics), Virgin Brides (a wedding dress retailer), and Virgin Cola (an attempt to take down Coke and Pepsi) were all shut down due to poor sales well before they risked bankruptcy. In 2014, Branson's spaceflight company Virgin Galactic faced a major setback with the malfunction and subsequent destruction of their VSS *Enterprise* spacecraft during a test flight. This high-profile disaster resulted in some setbacks to the spaceflight program, but Branson has forged ahead, and is now closer than ever to fulfilling his goal of taking paying customers to space.

Acumen aside, Branson has also had his share of luck. The first album he produced was Mike Oldfield's *Tubular Bells*, which went multiplatinum in the UK and became the theme song for *The Exorcist*. He then sold Virgin Records in 1992 for $1 billion to fund his fledgling airline—a move that seemed completely insane at the time, but looked downright visionary seven years later, as CD sales plummeted and the record industry fought the transition to digital. Branson might still be worth billions of dollars today if not for good fortune such as that, but there's no arguing that these two strokes of luck didn't greatly influence Virgin's health and success.

And what does Branson do with all that money? Aside from buying two islands in the Caribbean (which he promptly turned into luxury resorts in addition to his family's personal getaway—see, making money yet again), he is dedicated to philanthropy. Virgin Unite, the nonprofit arm of Virgin Group, funds a range of initiatives, from reducing carbon emissions to improving healthcare in Africa. With Nelson Mandela and Peter Gabriel, Branson founded the Elders, a group of established global leaders concerned with human rights issues worldwide. Members include Kofi Annan, Jimmy Carter, and Archbishop Desmond Tutu. Branson also founded the Branson Centre of Entrepreneurship, a networking and training program located in South Africa and Jamaica. Branson has been quick to speak out and form initiatives for national and global causes he believes in, and in 2000, he was knighted by the Prince of Wales for his services to entrepreneurship. He joined the B Team to plead with governments to reduce greenhouse emissions, started a pro-EU campaign to educate the British public on the implications of Brexit, and began using Virgin Orbit and Virgin Galactic to produce ventilators and oxygen hoods for patients of COVID-19.

Branson isn't afraid to fail, and he knows that in order to succeed, he must find and cultivate talented people. He's never followed the money, but the money has certainly followed him—and above everything, his focus remains squarely on having fun. Branson's unique style of business is captured in this book. It's an enlightening collection of quotes directly from the man himself. Have fun with it—he certainly would.

Part I

GUIDING PRINCIPALS

Entrepreneurship

I THINK ENTREPRENEURSHIP is our natural state—a big adult word that probably boils down to something much more obvious like "playfulness."

—*Business Stripped Bare*, page 39

BEING AN ENTREPRENEUR is one of life's greatest adventures, where you are always learning new things and growing.

—**"If you find business boring you're doing it wrong,"** ***Virgin*, November 13, 2017**

THE HEADMASTER CALLED me in one day and said, "either you leave school and run the magazine, or you stop running the magazine and stay at school," and so I said, "thank you for that choice—I'm off to run the magazine."

—*The Brave Ones*, **November 13, 2017**

SOMEBODY ELSE LAUGHED... "Why not Virgin? We're all virgins"—hysterical laughter all around. And I suddenly thought, "I am a virgin of business, I might be a virgin of other things as well, and why not Virgin?"

—*Bloomberg Game Changers*, **May 10, 2011**

REGARDING STARTING VIRGIN *Atlantic:* I'm not on a crusade with this thing.... If we had to pack it all in, the whole venture wouldn't cost but two months' profit of the Virgin Group.

—*Wall Street Journal*, **August 20, 1984**

I THINK AS much practical experience as people can have, the better... I'm dyslexic, so I know that I learn the most from practical experience. The more one can actually make a school act practically, the better.

—**"Richard Branson: Talking Management,"**
February 16, 2010

I have no secret. There are no rules to follow in business. I just work hard and, as I always have done, believe I can do it.

—*Screw It, Let's Do It*, page 30

WE WORKED OUT that there was no need for shops to be charging the amount they were for records, so we started a mail-order company that would sell any record, from any record manufacturer, for 10 percent to 25 percent less than their commercial price. For instance, we could buy a record from EMI for 31 shillings, which a shop would sell at 40 shillings. Instead, we sell it for 35 shillings. Virgin Records is helping hundreds and hundreds of young people throughout the country to get records at about 6 shillings cheaper—or 6 to 8 shillings cheaper—than they would anywhere else. At the same time, it's also starting up new groups who have been scorned by some of the big companies. And we're listening to their records and giving them a chance to get going themselves.

—**Unnamed documentary, 1971**

VIRGIN WOULD NOT be the company it is today if we had not taken risks along the way. You really do have to believe in what you are doing.

—Like a Virgin, page 27

ENTREPRENEURS HAVE THE dynamism to get something started.... Yet an entrepreneur is not necessarily good at the nuts and bolts of running a business.

—Business Stripped Bare, page 259

AS A SMALL-BUSINESS person, you must immerse yourself 100 percent in everything and learn about the ins and outs of every single department.... And as the business gets bigger, you will have to decide if you're a manager or an entrepreneur. If you're a manager you can stay with that business and help it grow. If you're an entrepreneur, you need to find a manager. Then you should move on, enjoy yourself and then set up your next enterprise.

—Business Stripped Bare, pages 260–261

WHO IS THE entrepreneur I most admire? Steve Jobs. He is the greatest comeback artist, he has twice been down and out and fought his way back and created a brilliant global company. Everything he does is real class. If he wanted to rename his company Virgin Apple I'm sure we would be more than happy to merge!

—Richard's Blog, March 30, 2011

THE ABILITY TO bounce back after a setback is probably the single most important trait an entrepreneurial venture can possess.

—Like a Virgin, page 61

ENTREPRENEURIAL BUSINESS FAVORS the open mind. It favors people whose optimism drives them to prepare for many possible futures, pretty much purely for the joy of doing so.

—Richard's Blog, December 26, 2012

WE'RE HAVING A board meeting, and I said something like, "Is that good news or bad news?" and one of the fellow directors said, "Look, Richard, just come outside a minute." And he said, "Look, I don't think you know the difference between 'net' and 'gross' yet." And I said, "Well, yeah, I sort of got away with it for the last 40 years."

—**"Richard Branson: Talking Management,"
February 16, 2010**

THE CHALLENGE IS to follow through on a great idea. I think if [you've] got a great idea, you need to just give it a try. And if you fall flat on your face, pick yourself up and try again. Learn from your mistakes. And, remember, you've got to go make a real difference in people's lives if you're going to be successful.

—*Success*, **July 1, 2009**

Entrepreneurship is also about excellence. Not excellence measured in awards or other people's approval, but the sort that one achieves for oneself by exploring what the world has to offer.

—*Success*, July 1, 2009

IT'S RARE FOR me or the team to consider only
the money that can be made. I feel it's pointless
to approach investing with the question, "How
can I make lots of money?"

—Like a Virgin, page 45

I'M NOT SURE that somebody will know that
they're an entrepreneur from the beginning. I
think they will have a desire to make a difference
[in] other peoples' lives, and they'll see that
something's frustrating them, there's a gap
in the market, they feel they can do it better
themselves, and they'll try to fill that gap in
the market. And then they almost become an
entrepreneur by default. I don't think you can set
out to become an entrepreneur. I think you've got
to set out to a make a difference to other peoples'
lives.

—I Love Marketing, July 8, 2011

I KNEW IF I could create the kind of airline I'd want to fly on that was exceptionally better than any other airline flying that it was likely that more money would come in in the year than go, and I'd have money left over at the end of the year, and that turned out to be the case because people loved Virgin Atlantic, they went out of their way to fly it, the planes were full. And at the end of the year, we ended up getting our second 747, and in the end of the next year, our third and fourth 747.

—"My approach to life," *In Depth with Graham Bensinger*, January 31, 2018

THERE IS NOTHING wrong with doing business with your friends—in fact, I encourage it.... [However, the] fact that your partner is also a friend cannot be an excuse for turning a blind eye.

—*Like a Virgin*, page 126

Entrepreneurship is all about taking risks—potentially disruptive and frightening life risks.

—"The difference between having an idea
and being an entrepreneur," *Virgin*, July 5,
2019

How the Sex Pistols were signed to Virgin Records: They were still signed to EMI and when I got back to the office, I rang up the chairman of EMI. I left a message with his secretary saying that if he wanted to get rid of this embarrassment, could he give me a ring. And the secretary gave me quite a curt response, saying that, you know, "We're quite happy with the Sex Pistols, thank you." That night the Sex Pistols went on the Bill Grundy show [called Today] and there were a number of swear words...and I got a call straight after the show saying the chairman himself was on the phone, and could I come over for a 6 o'clock breakfast the next morning, when he'd like to hand over the contract to us. So we ended up sort of getting the Sex Pistols by default.

—**"God Save the Queen—The Sex Pistols Interview,"**
September 27, 2012

I FOUND CONVENTIONAL schoolwork hopeless.... I decided at a very young age that I needed to get out of this environment and carve my own way in life.

—*Big Think*, June 2, 2011

FROM MY VERY first day as an entrepreneur, I've felt the only mission worth pursuing in business is to make people's lives better.

—"Richard Branson talks about his 'debilitating' shyness, climate change, and being a father," *Business Insider UK*, August 12, 2016

ANYONE CAN START up a new business from home. You can wash windows, take in ironing, or walk dogs. You can be an artist or a writer.... Even the Queen sells her farm produce from Windsor and Sandringham on the Web, as does Prince Charles with his Duchy Originals[.]

—*Screw It, Let's Do It*, pages 44–45

I do a lot by gut feeling and a lot by personal experience. I mean, if I relied on accountants to make decisions, I most certainly would have never gone into the airline business. I most certainly would not have gone into the space business, and I certainly wouldn't have gone into most of the businesses that I'm in. So, in hindsight, it seems to have worked pretty well to my advantage.

—*Success*, July 1, 2009

REGARDING A SIX-MONTH-LONG drop in profits on the US side of the business: We are investing for the future. We think for the long term, not the short term.

—*Billboard*, **June 4, 1988**

I SOMETIMES THINK that entrepreneurs have a lot in common with scouts for professional sports organisations. They are out there talent-spotting, whether with established stars on other teams or undiscovered, up-and-coming raw young talent that hasn't made it big as yet.

–*The Virgin Way: Everything I Know About Leadership*,
September 9, 2014

Business and

Investments

BUSINESS IS WHAT concerns us. If you care about something enough to do something about it, you're in business.

—*Richard's Blog*, September 25, 2012

I WANT TO build Virgin into the greatest entertainment group in the world.... Whatever we are doing in England, we can do in the rest of the world. We are in 17 countries worldwide and are growing very rapidly, with over two-thirds of our income from overseas.

—*Houston Chronicle*, July 4, 1980

...[A] FEW OPPORTUNITIES have slipped away. I had the chance to invest in Ryanair...I turned down the chance to invest in Trivial Pursuit and a wind-up radio.

—*Screw It, Let's Do It*, page 59

THE BEAUTY OF business is that it does not just have one single community.... The businesses that are most successful connect with everyone as an individual, not just as an order number or a transaction.

—*Screw Business As Usual*, page 299

REGARDING VIRGIN ATLANTIC'S inability to fly from London to Glasgow due to a lack of landing slots: It's absolutely bonkers and it makes me angry. We could have achieved so much more in this country [by] creating a massive number of jobs.

—*This Is Money*, April 13, 2013

IF A BANK or other investor is looking at your business, they have almost certainly looked at your competitors as well. In your presentation, therefore, it's imperative that you understand your competition and irreverently explain why your business will do better. Blow them away! Avoid being overly negative.

—*Like a Virgin*, **page 41**

PEOPLE SAID AT the time that we were mad to sell the record company to put the money into an airline. As it turns out, of course, the record industry's collapsed, and the airline industry hasn't done too badly for us.

—*Bloomberg Game Changers*, **May 10, 2011**

Business requires astute decision-making and leadership. It requires discipline and innovation. It also needs attitude, a good sense of humor, and, dare I say it, luck.

—*Business Stripped Bare*, page 7

Don't be afraid to take calculated risks. Sometimes they turn out to be less dangerous than the sure thing.

—*Like a Virgin,* page 59

REGARDING TOUGH TIMES at Virgin in 1976: ... [W]e cut back on whatever we could: we sold our cars, we closed down the swimming pool at the Manor [Virgin's recording studio], we cut down on the stock in the record shops, we didn't pay ourselves, we dropped a few artists from the record label, and [we] made nine staff redundant.

—*Losing My Virginity*, page 110

[RUPERT MURDOCH'S] EMPIRE should be looked at by competition authorities, and it should be decided if it's good for democracy that one person has so much influence.

—*Real Business*, July 14, 2011

REGARDING HIS 1971 arrest and conviction for tax evasion: Since then, I've made sure that we've done everything ethically, and without worry that someone's going to come knocking on our door.

—*Bloomberg Game Changers*, May 10, 2011

I try to keep bureaucracy to a minimum, and remind my teams that business, as well as life, should be fun.

—*Entrepreneur*, August 27, 2012

...Virgin America is a great airline and we're very proud of it.... We've been through 9/11, SARS—you name it. And fortunately, we've built up the financial capabilities to deal with these tough years. We're just having to tighten the belt until the good years come again.

—*Time*, September 1, 2009

Protecting the downside is critical. We'll make bold moves, but we'll also make sure we've got ways out if things go wrong.

—"Richard Branson: Talking Management," February 16, 2010

I rang up Boeing and I said, "My name's Richard Branson, and I'd like to buy a secondhand 747." And they said, "What did you say your company was called?" I said, "Virgin".... To give them credit they said, "OK look, we'll give you a go. As long as, unlike your name, your airline's going to go the whole way."

—Aspen Ideas Festival, July 5, 2007

REGARDING VIRGIN'S STATUS as a set of more than 300 separate private businesses: I think we've proved that a branded group of separate businesses, each with limited liability for its own financial affairs, makes sense. We're never going to have a Barings Bank situation where a rogue trader is able to bring down the whole Virgin Group.

—*Business Stripped Bare*, **pages 4–5**

WE VERY RARELY license the Virgin name per se, we normally start as either owning the company or a big share holder in the company. Then, maybe later on in the life of the company, once it's matured, we might sell it and then use the money to start new companies. The kinds of companies we go into are often areas where we're frustrated and feel it could be done better.

—**"Richard Branson: His Views On Entrepreneurship, Well-Being And Work Friendships,"** *Forbes*, **October 23, 2017**

There have been times I was almost bankrupt, and I was very glad to see my name in the *Sunday Times* "Rich List," because I thought it would assuage the bank manager. (The figures were often wildly off the mark both ways—but I wasn't complaining.)

—*Business Stripped Bare*, page 325

REGARDING THE PHRASE, *"The customer is always right":* It has endured because it sounds wonderful to marketers, but most established companies have learned from experience that it is way too all-encompassing to apply in everyday business. In truth, the customer is only right most of the time—after all, they're only human.

—*Like a Virgin*, page 63

THE MUSIC BUSINESS is a strange combination of real and intangible assets.... The rock business is a prime example of the most ruthless kind of capitalism.

—*Losing My Virginity*, page 61

I LOST FAITH in myself only once, and that was in 1986...I was told I should go public.... I no longer felt that I was standing on my own two feet. We doubled our profits, but Virgin shares started to slip and, for the first time in my life, I was depressed.

—*Screw It, Let's Do It*, pages 77–80

IN MANY WAYS, 1987, our year of being a public company, was Virgin's least creative year. We spent at least 50 percent of our time heading off to the City [London's financial district] to explain to fund managers, financial advisers, and City PR firms what we were doing, rather than just getting on and doing it.

—*Losing My Virginity*, page 185

FREEDOM IS SOMETHING worth paying for....
All that time and expense can now be put into dealing with our artists.

—*Billboard*, October 15, 1988

Over the years we've enjoyed taking on the big, fat, bloated companies and trying to turn them upside down...and I like to think we've done it in a fun way, rather than taking ourselves too seriously.

—*Allan Gregg in Conversation*, April 1, 2001

SINCE MIKE OLDFIELD was the first artist we signed, we had no idea what sort of a contract to offer him. Luckily, Sandy Denny, originally a singer with Fairport Convention who had now gone solo, had recently recorded at the Manor. She had become a friend of mine, and I asked her for a copy of her contract with Island Records. This was apparently a standard Island Records deal, and we retyped it word for word, changing "Island Records" to "Virgin Music," and "Sandy Denny" to "Mike Oldfield."

—Losing My Virginity, page 85

THE KEY TO success is unwavering commitment and focus. You will make mistakes as you launch your product or service — a ton of them. But keep your eye on the prize and never blink.

—"The difference between having an idea and being an entrepreneur," *Virgin*, July 5, 2019

Branding and Marketing

The Virgin brand is a guarantee that you'll be treated well, that you'll get a high-quality product which won't dent your bank balance, and you'll get more fun out of your purchase than you expected—whatever it is.... No other brand has become a "way-of-life" brand the way Virgin has.

—Business Stripped Bare, page 46

REGARDING SELECTING A celebrity guest to appear at a Virgin Megastore opening in NYC: It was either Marilyn Manson or the mayor, but we decided to pick Marilyn Manson...one was cooler.

—Late Night with Conan O'Brien, August 27, 1998

I GET UP well before we land to walk the aisles and say hello to our passengers. Showing my face is good for the brand; even more useful, I get to see for myself where we can improve and strengthen our service.

—Reach for the Skies, page 160

Getting every little bit of the design right is so important.... Great design can be great marketing.

—*Cool Hunting*, October 11, 2012

AFTER A MARKETING stunt gone wrong, in which Branson bungee jumped off the Palms Casino in Las Vegas, hit the side of the building, and split his pants: I've a few bumps and bruises. I never thought I could use the phrase "by the seat of my pants" so literally. But before anyone feels sorry for me, I did have Pamela Anderson waiting at the bottom to mop my brow.

—*Daily Mirror*, October 12, 2007

AS NICE AS it is to read articles that say the Virgin brand is one of the most powerful in the world, our corporate goal is to make it one of the most trusted.

—*Like a Virgin*, page 294

Publicity is absolutely critical. You have to get your brand out and about, particularly if you're a consumer-oriented brand.... A good PR story is infinitely more effective than a full-page ad, and a damn sight cheaper.

—*Business Stripped Bare*, page 63

MY ADVENTUROUS SIDE means that I don't get stuck behind a desk. I make sure that I spend most of my time out and about, talking to people, asking questions, making notes, and experiencing my businesses through the customer's eyes.

—Screw It, Let's Do It, page 156

...[B]RANDS ALWAYS MEAN something. If you don't define what the brand means, a competitor will. Apple's adverts contrasting a fit, happy, creative Mac with a fat, glum, nerdy PC tell you all you need to know about how that works. Even in the absence of competition, a betrayed brand can wreak a terrible revenge on a careless company. How many brands do you know mean "shoddy," "late," and "a rip-off"?

—Richard's Blog, October 7, 2008

I like to think [Virgin] stands for quality...

—TED Talks, March 2007

STRANGELY, I THINK my dyslexia has helped... for instance, when we're launching a new company, I need to be able to understand the advertising. If I understand the advertising, I believe that anybody out there can understand the advertising.

—*Time*, 2012

YOU COULDN'T BUY a quarter-page ad on the front of the *New York Times*, but when my sinking speedboat or crashing hot-air balloon just happened to feature the distinctive Virgin logo, there we were!

—*Like a Virgin*, page 35

BRITISH AIRWAYS WAS sponsoring this giant wheel [the ferris wheel known as the London Eye] on the other side of the House of Commons, and they were having technical problems getting the wheel up, and they had the world's press there to film it as it was going up. We had an airship [blimp] company so I scrambled this airship and...headed it towards this giant wheel, and as it flew over [its] massive banner at the back just simply said, "BA can't get it up." And we had a lot of great coverage at BA's expense for that. And the press loved it, and obviously that helped get Virgin on the map.

—*I Love Marketing*, July 8, 2011

I CAN'T SPEAK for other people, but dyslexia shaped my—and Virgin's—communication style. From the beginning, Virgin used clear, ordinary language. If I could quickly understand a campaign concept, it was good to go. If something can't be explained off the back of an envelope, it's rubbish.

—*Forbes*, October 22, 2012

Our people do it with style and panache. They have fun. They try to bring good value for money, they try to make sure that the quality is better than any other company around, and they try to do it ethically. So I think that when members of the public come in contact with the Virgin brand...they feel they can trust it, and I think people who work for the Virgin brand want to make sure they don't let the brand down.

— "Executive Insight: Richard Branson," *Think with Google,* September 2011

WE SOON FOUND that [social media] channels were an amazing tool for reaching our customers and the public. One of the first things we learned was that our new social media accounts gave us a real-time view of how we could improve.

—*CNBC*, **September 12, 2012**

REGARDING WHETHER CROSSING the world in a hot-air balloon was a good marketing tactic: I think our airline took a full page ad at the time, saying, "Come on, Richard, there are better ways of crossing the Atlantic."

—**TED Talks, March 2007**

WE HAVE NAILED Virgin's colors to the masts of many businesses, so every one of them must pull its weight with our customers.

—*Richard's Blog*, **October 7, 2008**

VIRGIN HAS MANAGED to be hip but not so hip that it disappears within itself. ...it's about getting all the little details right but not swamping people in the brand.

> —**"Virgin founder Sir Richard Branson: 'Humour has always been a big part of our marketing'", the *Drum*, May 30, 2017**

I'D LIKE TO have really sexy Virgin hotels in space where people can go and stay in pods, head off in little spaceships around the moon.

> —**"Richard Branson envisions 'sexy hotels' in space", *Mashable*, October 3, 2016**

Over the years the Virgin brand has earned the reputation of being bold and unafraid. Isn't it extraordinary how few brands communicate fearlessness?

—*Business Stripped Bare,* page 187

REGARDING HOW HE decides to launch a new business or product: There's no point in us going into something unless we can really shake up an industry, make a major difference; unless it's going to enhance the Virgin brand, if there's any danger of damaging the brand in any way, even if it's going to make us a lot of money—you know, cigarette companies or something like that—we just wouldn't do it. And because life's short, we want to enjoy the experience.

—**"Richard Branson: Talking Management,"**
February 16, 2010

I BEGAN LIFE as a journalist, and I've always been sensitive to the fact that getting free coverage is one thing; deserving it is quite another.

—*Reach for the Skies,* **page 36**

VIRGIN IS AN unusual brand. I mean, most brands specialize in one area.... Virgin is more of a way-of-life brand, and we like to look after people's needs throughout their lives, whether it's their health, or their train travel, or their airline travel, or their music, or so on. And it's very important if you are a way-of-life brand that you don't have, say, one company letting the other companies down. So we strive to be the best in every sector that we take on. We're, generally speaking, the underdog, which is actually a lot more fun than being the Goliath.... We have a lot of fun in what we do, we love to make a difference, and we love to tear down barriers.

—Interview by Tanya Beckett, August 28, 2008

Leadership and Management

WHEN I WAS 21, someone described Virgin as an "unprofessional professional organization," which for my money is just about the best backhanded compliment anyone in business could ever receive.

—*Business Stripped Bare*, page 28

IT'S IMPORTANT FOR the staff who work for Virgin to know that the wealth is going to be spent in a constructive way, and that's what we plan to do.

—Big Think, June 2, 2011

SOME PEOPLE MIGHT see Virgin's 50,000 employees as a cost to be managed, but I see 50,000 potential passionate brand ambassadors.

—OPEN Forum by American Express, June 9, 2011

I hate the descriptor "human resources," by the way...I call them "people departments."

—*HR*, July 12, 2010

PARTIES ARE A way of galvanizing teams and
allowing people to let their hair down. They have
to inclusive and encouraging, and then they are
an excellent way of bringing everyone together
and forging a great business culture.

—Business Stripped Bare, page 257

IN 2004, I did a program called *The Rebel
Billionaire* for Fox Television, where I was nice
to people and then had to whittle them down
to a winner. In one episode, I told a participant
[named Sam Heshmati that] we were going to be
the first to go over the Victoria Falls in a barrel....
A split second before we were due to plummet,
I shouted: "Stop! Hold on just one moment, I
want to show you something."So we got out. And
I showed young Sam the bottom of the falls. I
pointed at the rocks below. "Sam," I admonished
him, "you were 10 seconds from certain death.
You shouldn't blindly accept a leader's advice.
You've got to question leaders
on occasions."

—Richard's Blog, December 10, 2008

Too many people are hiding in dark rooms flipping through too many words on big screens. There's a reason why I avoid boardrooms. I'd rather spend time with people "in the field," where eye contact, genuine conviction, and trustworthiness are in full evidence.

—*Forbes*, October 22, 2012

THE ABILITY TO listen, and the willingness to stick your neck out and ask the obvious question, are criminally underrated business essentials.

—Business Stripped Bare, **page 267**

THERE'S A MACHISMO about the way some managers talk about hiring and firing that I find downright repugnant.... I think that you should only fire somebody as an act of last resort.

—Business Stripped Bare, **page 263**

OUR VIEW AT Virgin is that collective responsibility bonds teams, and having pride in your work is a far better driver than a hierarchical culture where the boss calls the shots.

—HR, **July 12, 2010**

IF WE'RE LOOKING for somebody to run one of our companies, we want to be sure that they're fantastic motivators of people; that they love people, genuinely; that they're looking for the best in people; that they praise people; that they never criticize people; that they treat the junior staff as importantly as their fellow directors, if not more importantly—and I think that's what sets a good company apart from a bad company.

—**"Richard Branson: Talking Management,"**
February 16, 2010

I LEAVE THE day-to-day problems to the other executives in the company's various London offices. It means I can spend my days investigating things.

—***Wall Street Journal,*** **August 20, 1984**

THE KEY FOR me is that in today's world, I do not think it is effective or productive to force your employees [to either work from home or in the office]. Choice empowers people and makes for a more content workforce.

—*Richard's Blog*, **March 4, 2013**

THE MOST IMPORTANT thing about running a company is to remember all the time what a company is. A company is simply a group of people. And as a leader of people, you have to be a great listener, you have to be a great motivator, [and] you have to be very good at praising and looking for the best in people.

—**Big Think, June 2, 2011**

Empowering employees so that they can make good decisions is one of an entrepreneur's most important tasks. This means that you must build a corporate comfort zone in which your people can confidently express themselves and display the courage of their own convictions.

—*Like a Virgin,* page 89

FOR AS MUCH as you need a strong personality to build a business from scratch, you must also understand the art of delegation. I have to be willing to step back now. I have to be good at helping people run the individual businesses—it can't just be me that sets the culture when we recruit people.

—*HR*, July 12, 2010

I HAVE ALWAYS found that an instant barometer to the state of any company's employee relations is the way their people use the words "we" and "they."... Managers and business leaders should watch for this tendency. A company where the staff overuse the word "they" is a company with problems. If employees aren't associating themselves with their company by using "we," it is a sign that people up and down the chain of command aren't communicating—and if that turns out to be the case, you'll usually find secondary problems throughout the company affecting everything from development to customer service.

—*Like a Virgin*, page 52

If you don't lead a healthy lifestyle, your productivity will be completely screwed

—"Richard Branson: His Views On Entrepreneurship, Well-Being And Work Friendships," October 23, 2017

WHAT IS A business? A business is its people. I can't change a spark plug on a 747 but I think I'm good at finding the right people, the best people, and giving them the freedom to do a good job. And the freedom to make mistakes—not in the engineering department, [but] in other departments!

—Interview by Tanya Beckett, August 28, 2008

IN AN ADDRESS to new employees of Virgin Atlantic: Who's a new Virgin? We're the only company that can offer you that.

—*A Day in the Life*, August 17, 2011

THE KEY TO effective people management is ensuring everyone has a little...people management in them. It isn't solely Angela's [Smith, Virgin's then-head of group people management] job to make our people's policies work at Virgin. It's everyone's responsibility. We have a [team of people] who are in essence the custodians of the Virgin people brand, ensuring there is consistency throughout the group in key values, behaviors, and policies. But each business has its own shareholders and management—this way, we concentrate on the job at hand rather than [being] part of some enormous, faceless conglomerate. The process and approach systems come from the people management principles, but the brands have a certain amount of freedom to do what they want to do.

—*HR*, July 12, 2010

Fear stops people from doing so many things. Don't be afraid to talk to people you don't know, or try a new skill. They are probably just as nervous inside, and if you make the effort, people will often surprise you with a warm welcome.

—"My top tips for trying new things," *Virgin*, January 16, 2020

WE WENT FROM being a record business into starting an airline, [and] people thought we were mad.... Somebody from the entertainment business running an airline might not be such a bad thing [however], because not only can we find the right people to make sure it runs safely, but we can also find people to entertain our passengers, and they can actually have a pleasant journey.

—**Interview by Tanya Beckett, August 28, 2008**

FROM A YOUNG age, if I ever criticized somebody, my parents would make me go and stand in front of the mirror, and they just said, "Look, it's a bad reflection on yourself." Ever since then, in particular if you're running a company, you've just got to look for the best in everybody.... I think if you deal well with people, people will come back and deal with you again.

—**Interview by Michael Buerk, July 3, 2011**

VIRGIN DOES WORK very well without me...
when my balloon bursts, Virgin will continue to
flourish.

—Big Think, June 2, 2011

COMPANIES NEED TO have a lot more flexibility
with their people.... If somebody wants to golf
around the world for 2 months, okay, well, maybe
on an unpaid basis, let them do it. That sort of
flexibility I think is incredibly important because
most of our time, we spend at work.

—"Richard Branson: Talking Management,"
February 16, 2010

WE'VE ALWAYS HAD, at our core, a focus on our people and making sure that they are empowered to make decisions and feel part of a company that stands for something beyond making money. I've always believed that by taking care of people in my companies, the rest will take care of itself. This can be something simple, like allowing people to job-share or giving them the chance to run their own show. This has worked for us and has also built a pretty special group of people around the world who are not only passionate about Virgin, but also about making a difference in the world.

—Screw Business as Usual, **page 17**

WAY TOO MANY executives check their smartphones throughout meetings and during their off-hours. Apart from the fact that it's tantamount to rudeness in a meeting, it isn't good for anyone's concentration and has a negative impact on decision-making.

—Like a Virgin, **page 107-108**

IF IT DOESN'T come from the top down, people from below have got to shake the people at the top.... I think it's important for leaders to not worry about being seen to let your hair down, not worry about going out and getting drunk with your staff.

—"Richard Branson: Talking Management,"
February 16, 2010

IN THE EARLY days of Virgin, one of our people nicknamed me 'Dr Yes'. It was a friendly (I hope) dig at my perpetual eagerness to go along with trying new ideas.

–*The Virgin Way: Everything I Know About Leadership*,
September 9, 2014

THE VIRGIN WAY of managing our business is all about maintaining and promoting that almost childish curiosity level in our people to ensure they are never accepting of the status quo and always looking for new ways to improve upon it.

–*The Virgin Way: Everything I Know About Leadership*,
September 9, 2014

IN BUSINESS, IF one of our companies is failing, we take steps to identify and solve the problem. What we don't do is continue failing strategies that cost huge sums of money and make the problem worse.

—"Why it's time for drug regluation," CNN, September 8, 2014

IF YOU TAKE care of your employees, they will take care of your business.

— *The Washington Post*, June 10, 2015

VIRGIN IS ALL about fun, entertainment, [and] not taking ourselves too seriously.

—"Richard Branson No Longer Casino Virgin, Billionaire Buys Hard Rock Las Vegas to Add to Hotel Group," Casino.org, April 2, 2018

BUSINESS, AFTER ALL, is like a giant game of
chess: you have to make strategic moves, and
learn quickly from your mistakes.

> —"Stop playing it safe," *Virgin*, October 10, 2018

IT'S ALSO IMPORTANT to be able to have fun at
work – we spend so much of our lives working,
we need to be able to laugh along the way.

> —"Be the same at home as at work," *Virgin*, January 11,
> 2018

Part II

LOOKING TO THE FUTURE

Innovation

WHEN I STARTED Virgin 40 years ago, I wanted the change the relationship that customers had with companies.

—"**Virgin Mobile Presents: Our Higher Calling™**,"
March 14, 2012

IF YOUR BUSINESS proposition is innovative, your ultimate goal has to be "The customer always thinks that we are right."

—*Like a Virgin*, **page 66**

THE BEST, MOST solid way out of a crisis in a changing market is through experiment and adaptation.

—*Richard's Blog*, **November 27, 2008**

I seem to have spent my life—in the aviation business and elsewhere—separating the Things Not Done Because They Don't Work from the Things Not Done Because We Don't Do Them.

—*Reach for the Skies*, page 157

...[C]OMPLEXITY SOON GUMS up the works of an organization as it expands....The separation of day-to-day business from the motive energy that birthed the company does cause problems. Suddenly, innovating is seen as something extra, something special, something separated from the activities the company normally engages in. This is when niggles become endemic, intractable problems; morale declines; and the business begins to lose its way in the market place.

—*Business Stripped Bare*, page 216

REGARDING THE LAUNCH of Virgin Pulse, a line of personal electronics that was shut down after two years due to poor sales: Virgin loves to compete, especially in sectors where we feel people have been overcharged. We thought, "We can develop a range of electronics that are stylish and for which we're not charging too much." Virgin has a strong brand and we feel we can give other companies a run for their money.

—*USA Today*, October 14, 2003

So, if things don't work out, don't hesitate: Take that escape hatch. That way, when all's said and done, you will be able to gather your team, discuss what did or did not happen, and then embark on your next venture together. Not much older, but a lot wiser.

—*Like a Virgin,* page 47

WHEN ASKED HOW he could make air travel so inexpensive: That was just what they asked when I started selling records 20 percent cheaper than anyone else. We went from mail order to basement record stores, then bought a manor near Oxford where bands could play and started producing. The present airlines have just built up too big an overhead.

—*New York Times*, **April 10, 1984**

I LOOK AT it like this: if the automobile industry only produced Ferraris, that wouldn't be a great thing. It is nice to have an industry that makes something for everybody.

—**"Space, Satellites and Tea: An Interview with Richard Branson,"** *Satellite Digital*, **July 2018**

PROBABLY THE GREATEST frontier of opportunity is the creation of businesses that protect and harness our natural resources—with the obvious added benefit of reducing our carbon output.

—*Screw Business as Usual*, **page 205**

THE INTERNET HAS saved the airline business a boatload of money over the years. We were paying 7 to 10 percent commission on every ticket to the travel agents. Cutting the agents out of the business was liberating.

—Reach for the Skies, page 181

I THINK THAT the death knell of record labels is pretty well upon us. I had a wonderful time running Virgin Records some years ago, and discovering bands, it was tremendously exciting...but I think that time has moved on and I think record companies are almost a thing of the past.

—Digg Dialogg, May 4, 2009

INNOVATION CAN OCCUR when the most elementary questions are asked and employees are given the resources and power to achieve the answers.

—Business Stripped Bare, page 220

I'M INQUISITIVE, I can't say no. I keep on saying yes, and sometimes I suspect I've been doing that too often, but it has made life far more interesting than it would have been to have kept saying no.

—"Richard Branson discusses space travel, AI, and his friendship with Obama," *Business Insider*, October 9, 2017

BEING UNDER PRESSURE often brings out the best in people.

—"Performing best under pressure," *Virgin*, December 16, 2013

Not everybody is cut out to be an entrepreneur. But that doesn't mean you can't still come up with new ideas working within an organization. This is where intrapreneurs come in: They unleash the power of innovation from inside companies.

—*Richard's Blog*, November 11, 2012

I THINK LOW-EARTH Orbit (LEO) satellites...are a great complement to geostationary satellites and ground networks. In addition to providing more data to the bandwidth-hungry world we live in, it is particularly important as they can help the people that need it the most. It is relatively easy to get an internet connection in a big city in the United Kingdom or the United States. But, it is not practical to bring out cables into remote areas of the world. Those are the people that can really benefit from the same connectivity that the rest of us can enjoy.

—"Space, Satellites and Tea: An Interview with Richard Branson," *Satellite Digital*, July 2018

VIRGIN'S SUCCESS IS not down to its crystal-clear vision of the future. If it were, you'd be Virgining our company valuations on the Internet rather than Googling them—and our Megastores would have been sold off in the eighties.

—*Business Stripped Bare*, page 126

REGARDING THE 1984 movie Electric Dreams, which was produced by Virgin Films: Our publishing company is publishing the book, our distribution company is distributing the film, our record company is putting out the record, our video-game company is putting out the video game, and our video company is putting out the video.... Our studios recorded them, and our shops will be selling them. That's how we maximize profit.

—*Wall Street Journal*, **August 20, 1984**

ONE OF THE most amazing things about being dyslexic is the imagination it gives you. I started dreaming from a young age and then began trying to turn those dreams into reality

—**Twitter, February 13, 2020**

REGARDING THE DECISION to launch Virgin Cola:
Why should Coca-Cola forever be so dominant?
Just the fun of trying to take a bit of that market
share away from them, I found, was irresistable.
Everybody said it would be impossible, and
to an extent, we haven't had the same sort of
success [as] we've had with things like the airline
business. But we still sold a couple billion cans of
cola, and amongst young people in the countries
where we've launched it, we managed to keep the
youth image...which has been quite important.

—Allan Gregg in Conversation, April 1, 2001

MAKING CHANGES AND improvements
is a natural part of business, and for sole
[proprietorships] and very small companies, the
distinction between innovation and day-to-day
delivery is barely noticeable and unimportant.
It's all just business, and creative, responsive,
flexible business comes easier to you the smaller
your operation [is].

—*Richard's Blog*, November 27, 2008

When we lose touch of our intuition, we naturally become more risk-averse and conservative. At Virgin, we like to work fast, to try ideas, see if they stick, and find new solutions and new innovations if they don't.

—"Instinct in a world of analytics," *Virgin*, November 27, 2019

OVER THE YEARS we've pioneered comfortable reclining seats, flat beds, lounges with hairstylists and masseuses, and a motorcycle-and-limo home pickup service. Virgin Atlantic was the first to provide personal video screens in every seatback so our travelers could choose the films and television shows they wanted to watch. These are some of the ideas that worked. There were plenty that didn't. Does anyone remember our live in-flight entertainment?

—*Reach for the Skies*, page 158

I'VE FOUND THAT life's a lot more fun when you say yes than when you say no. Sometimes you fall flat on your face when you do it that way, but sometimes you got to make a decision, get on, and give it a go and you have to be a little bit brave and maybe even foolish when you do that and fortunately we've gotten away with it more often than we haven't.

—The Brave Ones, November 13, 2017

WITHOUT AMBITIOUS PEOPLE dreaming of a better future, innovation would end and progress would falter.

—"The importance of ambition," *Virgin*, April 10, 2014

Air and Space

MOST PEOPLE HANKER for a view of Earth from space. I should know: I'm one of them.

—*Reach for the Skies*, page 20

I SPEND A great deal of my life on airplanes. I'm sometimes exhausted by the routine, as much as the next business traveler. But there isn't a flight [that] goes by when I don't stare out of the window and thank my stars for what I'm seeing and feeling.

—*Reach for the Skies*, page 10

One of the most difficult and exciting challenges of running an airline—and it amazes me how few airlines take it seriously—is how to maintain the glamour of air travel.

—*Reach for the Skies,* page 158

OUR PLAN WAS to travel on to Puerto Rico—
but when we got to the airport, the flight was
canceled and people were roaming about, looking
lost. No one was doing anything. So I did—
someone had to. Even though I hadn't a clue what
I was really doing, with a great deal of aplomb I
chartered a plane for $2,000 and divided that by
the number of passengers. It came to $39 a head.
I borrowed a blackboard and wrote on it: VIRGIN
AIRWAYS. $39 SINGLE FLIGHT TO PUERTO
RICO. All the tickets were snapped up by grateful
passengers. I managed to get two free tickets out
of it and even made a small profit! The idea for
Virgin Airways was born, right in the middle of a
holiday, although the actual airline only properly
took off when I was sent a business idea some
years later.

—*Screw It, Let's Do It*, **pages 39–40**

I HAVE NO complaint with extra security [post-9/11]; I just don't understand why it has to be done so shoddily. You want to take my mother's knitting needles away? Okay, but why can I still buy a glass bottle full of flammable liquid once I get past security?

—*Reach for the Skies*, pages 158–159

INITIALLY, I WAS very skeptical, but then we looked at the figures. There's an enormous demand from people who want to fly to America cheaply.

—*New York Times*, June 3, 1984

I DO FIND it very strange that America is very service-[oriented], but the American airline industry is so anti-customer, and so uncomfortable, and really [seems] to herd people on and off like cattle. I think the government has had a hand in that by propping up the largest airlines; they've turned into quite weak companies.

—*USA Today*, October 14, 2003

I MEAN, WHEN we started 30 years ago with one plane flying out of England, there were 15 American carriers that we were competing with: Pan Am, TWA, Eastern, People Express, etc., etc. Every single one of them...disappeared. And they disappeared because, although we were much smaller than them, their quality was awful.

—NPR interview, October 10, 2012

Every day, the industry ties one and a half million people down in narrow metal tubes for hours at a time and insists that they do exactly what they're told. For the sake of everyone's safety, we must never forget that we're asking a hell of a lot from human nature.

—*Reach for the Skies*, page 159

THE MAJORITY OF your customers are going to be traveling in your economy class cabins, and it's extremely unwise not to look after them.

—Firstpost, October 26, 2012

THE AIRLINE BUSINESS is a strange one in that the American government keeps on jumping in and propping up these ghastly big airlines that offer the consumer next to nothing...I just hope they don't do it again!

—Interview by Tanya Beckett, August 28, 2008

WE ARE MAKING fantastic progress on Virgin Galactic's preparations for travel to space. It has been an amazing, [and] at times agonizing, process to get the space program this far, and as the weeks and months pass, we are steadily witnessing more little bits of history.

—Richard's Blog, March 5, 2013

REGARDING GALACTIC TRAVEL: If you've got a mother-in-law, we can always sort out one-way tickets.

— **Aspen Ideas Festival, July 5, 2007**

VIRGIN GALACTIC'S JOB is to [take] the incredible intellectual achievements and acts of personal heroism we've seen lighting up the skies of Mojave [where Virgin Galactic's research facility is located] and elsewhere and turn them into a business.

—***Reach for the Skies,*** page 283

I've always held [on] to the notion that you only live once, and that if you want your life to have any meaning, you simply have to throw yourself into things.

—*Reach for the Skies,* page 35

UP UNTIL NOW, flying into space has been like flying into aerial combat: There really has been no sure expectation that you're going to come down again in one piece. Virgin Galactic's launch system will change all that. Our launch system HAS to change all that, or space will be forever out of bounds. No ordinary people will ever go there. Most won't want to. Those who do want to will never be able to afford it.

—*Reach for the Skies*, page 316

REGARDING WHAT HIS first words would be in space: Something like, "space is now Virgin territory."

—*Condé Nast Traveler*, July 13, 2010

Would I have been happy without my successes in business? I'd like to think so. But... it depends on what you mean by "business." Would I have been happy had I not found concerns to absorb me and fascinate me and engage me every minute of my life? No, absolutely not, I'd be as miserable as sin.

—*Business Stripped Bare,* page 4

THE REGULATORS, FOR their part, have been tearing their hair out trying to make this work: Virgin Galactic—a private company that will fly an international clientele around on rockets over US territory—is a project to boggle the legal mind. The United States is the only country on earth where such a project could be made real.

—Reach for the Skies, pages 316–317

WE HAVE ONE planet in our solar system that's habitable and that's the Earth, and space travel can transform things back here for the better. First of all by just having people go to space and look back on this fragile planet we live on. People have come back transformed and have done fantastic things. There's a wonderful book called The Overview Effect, which has interviews with all the people who've been to space and [tells of] their experiences, and how it's changed them. I look forward to being changed in a positive way.

— **"Richard Branson: 'Millions of people would love to become astronauts'",** *The Guardian,* **April 10, 2016**

[GETTING TO MARS] is an incredible challenge, and I suspect Elon [Musk] will get there first. He's more interested in big rockets going big distances...my love for space is about how much it can do for people back here on earth.

— "Richard Branson discusses space travel, AI, and his friendship with Obama," *Business Insider*, October 9, 2017

WE'RE THEN LOOKING at seeing whether we can develop flights from New York to Australia in half an hour. It may be unbelievable, but that's the next stage.

— Aspen Ideas Festival, July 5, 2007

REGARDING WHETHER HE regrets his sense of adventure: I got pulled out of the sea I think six times by helicopters, and each time I didn't expect to come home to tell the tale, so in those moments you certainly wonder what you're doing up there.

—TED Talks, March 2007

I assumed, having seen the moon landing, that I would be able to go into space in my lifetime, because I was...a teenager at the time. But, you know, decade by decade went by, [and] NASA [wasn't] opening their doors to you and me. So I thought NASA needed some competition.

—Aspen Ideas Festival, July 5, 2007

REGARDING HIS PASSION for hot air balloons: If you want to escape the world entirely, it's all you need. Nobody can trouble you. Nobody can stop you.... You're not in control.

—*Reach for the Skies*, page 25

REGARDING A RIDE in an out-of-control balloon, and gathering the courage to jump out of it and into the ocean: It was a very, very lonely few moments.

—**TED Talks, March 2007**

Part III

VALUES

Personal

...GEORGE CLOONEY ONCE let slip that he'd swap his life for mine—much to the excitement of my wife!

—*Business Stripped Bare*, page 4

IN RESPONSE TO the question, "Who would play you in the film about your life?": Brad Pitt. He's handsome, sports a good beard, and is a great actor.

—*The Guardian*, April 2, 2010

I DON'T KNOW why the tie was ever invented. It's about one of the few things that Britain has exported successfully and it completely destroyed those lovely robes that the Japanese used to wear, and now everyone looks the same and dresses the same. I often have a pair of scissors in my top pocket to go cutting people's ties off.

—*Bloomberg Businessweek*, March 7, 2012

I'm definitely a "glass nearly full" kind of person rather than a "glass half full," so I think out of being just a generally positive person, you can make positive things happen.

—"My approach to life," *In Depth with Graham Bensinger*, January 31, 2018

You don't need much money to be happy...as long as you can have one breakfast, one lunch, one dinner; as long as you can sort out your family if they're ill.

—Digg Dialogg, **May 4, 2009**

Remember to have fun. There is no point in being in business if it is not fun.

—Like a Virgin, **page 20**

My colleagues know me as Dr. Yes because I find it hard to say no to new ideas and proposals.

—The Guardian, **April 2, 2010**

REGARDING BUYING NECKER Island in 1977: I asked him the price. "Three million pounds," he said. It was far beyond my reach. "I can offer £150,000," I said.... Three months later, I got a call to say the island was mine if I offered £180,000.

—*Screw It, Let's Do It*, pages 39–40

I BOUGHT [NECKER Island] when I was in my twenties.... It's a little jewel. It's the place that we escape to.

—*Digg Dialogg*, May 4, 2009

REGARDING THE FIRE that destroyed Branson's Necker Island home on August 22, 2011: It's at moments like these one realizes how unimportant "stuff" is.

—*Screw Business as Usual*, page x

REGARDING ADDING BEDROOMS to Virgin planes, which didn't actually happen: You can do it in boats, you can do it in your home, why shouldn't you be able to do it on planes?

—*Late Night with Conan O'Brien*, **August 27, 1998**

I HATE BEING out of control…. I prefer to have a great time and to keep my wits about me.

—*Losing My Virginity*, **page 66**

JUST THE OTHER day [my mother] said: "If you throw yourself around, a new hip is the price you pay. The old one looks like a door knocker, so I am going to use it as one." That quote sums up her spirit. She has actually had three new hips and has come back fighting every time. She is, and always has been, a fantastic example to our family.

—*Richard's Blog*, **March 26, 2013**

Money's only interesting for what it lets you do. On paper, if I was to sell up my shareholdings in the companies tomorrow, I would have considerable wealth. But where would be the fun in that?

—*Business Stripped Bare*, page 326

THERE IS A very thin dividing line between success and failure.

—Big Think, June 2, 2011

I THINK IT'S perhaps quite personal. I just love learning. I love challenging myself. I love challenging the people around me. If I see something that's not being done very well, I'll try to do it better.

—Interview by Michael Buerk, July 3, 2011

I DO SEEM to have conceived almost every way known to man to try to kill myself, and I've been very fortunate to be here today to talk about some of these stories.

—*Bloomberg Game Changers,* May 10, 2011

Those who know me, know I'm passionate about lists and top of my list of priorities is my family. My wife Joan and I do not consider our legacy to our children to be wealth or fame, but the opportunity to pursue happiness by following their own path.

—"Richard Branson talks about his 'debilitating' shyness, climate change, and being a father," *Business Insider UK*, August 12, 2016

THE IDEA OF board meetings horrifies me.

—*New York Times*, June 3, 1984

PART THREE *Personal*

I WAS 15 when I made the name of the company, I was 16 when I actually did it.

—*Late Night with Conan O'Brien*, August 27, 1998

REGARDING THE UTILITY of knighthood: I suppose if you're having problems getting a booking at a restaurant or something, it might be worth using.

—**TED Talks, March 2007**

I'VE ALWAYS BELIEVED in befriending your enemies.

—*Wall Street Journal*, April 22, 2012

RICHARD BRANSON IN HIS OWN WORDS   121

If you go into a conversation with your mind already made up, you may as well not bother.

—"Want to be a distruptor? Keep an open mind," *Virgin*, April 23, 2015

DO YOU REMEMBER when you turned 21? Yours truly was trying to get our record label off the ground, living on a houseboat, and—most importantly—having far too much fun to remember it all too clearly.

—*Richard's Blog*, March 7, 2013

I, FOR ONE, would far rather be a nice guy, working with great people, having fun with a small successful business, than a miserable guy heading up a hugely profitable multinational mega-corp. But that's your call.

—*Like a Virgin*, page 21

[RETIRING] SEEMS VERY boring.

—*Forbes*, February 14, 2013

I DON'T WORK for the money. It's all done out of natural interest and enthusiasm, rather than commercial hard-headedness.

—*Houston Chronicle*, July 4, 1980

I'VE TRAINED MYSELF out of a slight shyness....
I used to find it difficult to deal with public
speaking.

—Interview by Michael Buerk, July 3, 2011

THERE WAS A great sense of teamwork within
our family. Whenever we were within Mum's
orbit, we had to be busy. If we tried to escape by
saying that we had something else to do, we were
firmly told we were selfish. As a result, we grew
up with a clear priority of putting other people
first.

—*Losing My Virginity*, page 20

PERHAPS IT WAS dyslexia that drove me to be entrepreneurial in the first place, because I knew instinctively that I'd never pass exams and go into a profession, such as the law, as my father and his father before him had. I'd never be a teacher, a doctor, or a banker—or so I thought. Ideas and good schemes to set up a business that didn't require much formal learning seemed to be one of my best options.

—Screw Business as Usual, page 55

I HAVE ALWAYS loved the question, "How old would you be if you didn't know how old you are?" My answer to that would be "in my twenties"...

—Screw Business as Usual, page 13

SCREW IT, JUST get on and do it.

—Interview by Michael Buerk, July 3, 2011

I'M DYSLEXIC SO I was hopeless at conventional schooling.

—*The Brave Ones*, November 13, 2017

I REMEMBER WALKING around the garden with my dad. The first time I walked around, he tried to persuade me out of [leaving school], then the second time around, he said, "Look, if you've really made up your mind—On reflection, when I left college at 22, I had no idea what I wanted to do; you're 15, you know what you want to do, so give it a go and if it doesn't succeed we'll try to get you an education again."

—*The Brave Ones*, November 13, 2017

MY APPRACH TO life is to not take life too seriously, but I think that's important to balance things and if in the process we can make people smile a bit, why not?

—**Creating Climate Wealth Workshops Summit,
Singapore, May 13, 2013**

I'm talking about the power of the ordinary, everyday person to become entrepreneurs and change-makers, to set up their own businesses, to seek their own fortune and be in control of their own lives, to say— screw business as usual, we can do it! We can turn things upside down and make a huge difference.

—*Screw Business as Usual,* page 6

WHEN I WAS a boy my parents never let me spend my time watching television. I well remember one time when my mum turned the TV off and asserted that it was going to be 'the death of conversation', which immediately provoked a twenty-minute argument with her TV-starved son. After we'd agreed to disagree, Mum couldn't resist getting the last word in: 'You see, if you'd been watching TV we wouldn't just have enjoyed that interesting discussion.' And, while I may not have appreciated it at the time, my mother was absolutely correct.

—*The Virgin Way: Everything I Know About Leadership*,
September 9, 2014

ONE OF THE most resounding lessons I learned from my father was the importance of dreaming.

—Twitter, March 10, 2020

Some of our best employees at Virgin are people who've been in prison, including myself.

—"Second Chances,"
TEDxIronwoodStatePrison, May 29, 2014

I OFTEN MAKE up my mind about someone
within 30 seconds of meetings them. When I
met Joan 44 years ago today, it was love at first
sight

—**Twitter, February 7, 2020**

I OWE A lot to my wife Joan – from inspiring
the names of record-breaking albums to finding
our home on Necker Island and raising our two
wonderful children.

—**Twitter, February 7, 2020**

LEARNING FROM FAILURE builds character, and
teaches us so much more than not trying ever
will.

—**"My advice to parents? Let your children fail,"** *Virgin*,
May 12, 2017

Dyslexia is just a different way of thinking, not a disadvantage. Wouldn't the world be rather boring if we were all the same?

—Twitter, February 13, 2020

Social

Responsibility

THERE IS SUCH a thing as enlightened self-interest, and we should encourage it. It is possible to turn a profit while making the world a better place.

—Business Stripped Bare, page 289

I LEARNED TO grasp opportunities and the nettle with equal passion. I learned that if you see a bright idea—go with it. If you see a problem—deal with it. Do good, don't do harm. Give back if you can. *Editor's note: "Grasp the nettle" is a British idiom that means "tackle a problem decisively."*

—Screw Business as Usual, page 57

FOR A RELATIVELY small amount of money, you can make a big difference to a lot of people's lives.

—Big Think, June 2, 2011

TOO MANY BUSINESSPEOPLE say things like,
"They really should do something about
developing alternative fuels." Well, we decided
we simply couldn't wait for "them," and picked
up the ball ourselves.

—*Like a Virgin*, page 119

WHEN ASKED, "WHAT *would your super power
be?" Branson responded*: To be able to save our
planet.

—*The Guardian*, April 2, 2010

CAN SUSTAINABILITY BE sexy? I think so!

—**Twitter, November 20, 2016**

We know, for sure, that human beings are changing the climate. This surely can't come as a surprise. What other species do you know that starts fires?

—*Reach for the Skies*, page 265

VIRGIN GALACTIC AND its partner, Scaled Composites, are creating a lot of jobs in a town [Mojave] where they are a scarce commodity, and in a region that currently has a 4 percent higher unemployment rate than the rest of California.

—*Richard's Blog*, December 10, 2009

I LOVE BEES because I think that the beehive is a metaphor for the world. Every member of the community is of equal value, although they have different tasks.

—*Screw Business as Usual*, page 220

TO CUT OFF the flow of money to the top criminals, all we have to do is call a halt to the drug war and decrminialize the use of illegal substances.

—*Like a Virgin*, page 79

Taking bold action on climate change simply makes good business sense. . . . It's also the right thing to do for people and the planet.

—"Richard Branson leads call to free global economy from carbon emissions," *The Guardian*, February 5, 2015

...[W]E HAVE SET up the Branson School of Entrepreneurship [now called the Centre of Entrepreneurship] to help foster budding entrepreneurs and their fledgling companies. Most of our students are young men and women, determined to study hard and build their businesses. One of the most important things we impart to them is the importance of enjoying [their] work.

—Open Forum by American Express, August 27, 2010

I WAS SITTING in the bath when it occurred to me: Why not just divert all the profits made by the Virgin Group from our carbon-creating businesses—such as the airlines and trains—and invest it in developing the cleaner technologies of the future?

—*Business Stripped Bare*, pages 309–310

THE WAR ON drugs has caused so much misery in the world, [and] it's been going on for 40 years; if we'd had a business that had failed for one year, we would have changed tack or we would have closed it down.

—**LinkedIn, December 11, 2012**

CAPITALISM IS THE only system that works, but it has its flaws; for one, it brings great wealth to only a few people. That wealth obviously brings extreme responsibility.

—*O* **magazine, December 1, 2007**

A BASIC INCOME should be introduced in Europe and in America....It's a disgrace to see people sleeping on the streets with this material wealth all around them.

—*New York Times*, **June 29, 2018**

BASIC INCOME IS going to be all the more important. If a lot more wealth is created by AI, the least that the country should be able to do is that a lot of that wealth…goes back into making sure that everybody has a safety net.

—"Richard Branson discusses space travel, AI, and his friendship with Obama," *Business Insider*, October 9, 2017

THE SMALLER WE make the world, the more we have to cherish its richness and diversity.

—*Reach for the Skies*, page 161

I CONSTANTLY MEET a growing army of entrepreneurs around the world, and when they ask me if I have one single message which will help them, I tell them it's this: Doing good can help improve your prospects, your profits, and your business; and it can change the world.

—*Screw Business as Usual*, page 2

WE MUST STOP criminalizing drug users. Health and treatment should be offered to drug users—not prison. Bad drug policies affect literally hundreds of thousands of individuals and communities across the world. We need to provide medical help to those that have problematic use—not criminal retribution.

—*Richard's Blog*, December 19, 2011

THOSE OF US who have been fortunate enough to acquire wealth must play a role in looking at how we use these means to make the world a far better place. It's not about martyrdom, it's about balance and compassion and figuring out how we can build new ways to live together, as a truly global village, that allow everyone to prosper.

—*Screw Business as Usual*, page 6

THE TECHNOLOGY EXISTS for fracking to work effectively, but it is up to industry to show leadership and prove they can do fracking safely. It is also up to policy makers to ensure they regulate fracking as responsibly as possible, with accurate pricing.... Gas is much cleaner than coal and oil, and global warming is the number one issue facing the modern world.

—Richard's Blog, **February 18, 2013**

A FEW YEARS ago, I was enjoying a nice bath at home, in warm water and soft lighting...you can imagine how excited I got as Al Gore walked me through his *Inconvenient Truth* slide show!

—Forbes, **October 22, 2012**

ON BRANSON'S TERM for social entrepreneurship:
So, what on earth does that [Capitalism 24902] mean? Well, we started talking about how the name had to capture the new level of responsibility that each of us had for others in the global village, and how this needed to be a movement that went beyond a handful of businesses or one country. When someone mentioned that the circumference of the earth is 24,902 miles, Capitalism 24902 was born! Very simple really...every single business person has the responsibility for taking care of the people and planet that make up our global village, all 24,902 circumferential miles of it.

—Screw Business as Usual, page 19

I WAS ON the phone this morning with the president of the Maldives—there's been a coup there, and I'm trying to see if I can help him not get arrested. I'm in a position where I can make a difference, and think I shouldn't waste that.

—Entrepreneur, June 19, 2012

I AM NOT a believer in just handing out checks; you should run charity like a business driving change. That is, I believe that most people, even the poorest and most deprived, don't just want to be told what's good for them; they want to be involved in helping to make their own lives better.

—*Screw Business as Usual*, page 33

NRA, NRA, HOW many kids have you killed today?

—*Richard's Blog*, March 20, 2013

When somebody slips up, they should be given a chance. It's not only the right thing to do, but I think it's the right thing for society as well. And instead, in America, when people come out of prison, they continue to be punished... Which puts people on the path to reoffending again.

—"Second Chances," TEDxIronwoodStatePrison, May 29, 2014

WHAT WE'RE TRYING to do thorugh the Carbon War Room is take a different approach. You know, I'm a businessman, I've got airlines, I've got spaceships companies, I've got train companies; I put out tons and tons of carbon, and most people in this world come from industries so we're all putting out a lot of carbon. It is in our interests as business people to come up with fun, imaginitive ways of reducing our carbon output without damaging our companies.

> —Creating Climate Wealth Workshops Summit,
> Singapore, May 13, 2013

WE DON'T LIVE forever and it'd be lovely if we could leave the world in as nice a world for our children, our grandchildren.

> —Creating Climate Wealth Workshops Summit,
> Singapore, May 13, 2013

WE NEED TO find real world solutions which benefit everyone. I've been very passionate about renewable energy for many years, particularly solar energy and its capacity to bring abundant clean, sustainable energy to millions around the globe.

—"Richard Branson talks about his 'debilitating' shyness, climate change, and being a father," *Business Insider UK*, August 12, 2016

IF WE CAN get every business in the world to adopt a global problem, get slightly smaller businesses to adopt a national problem, get smaller businesses still to adopt local problems, then we can get on top of pretty well every problem in the world.

—"Richard and Holly Branson: A Father-Daughter Conversation," *the New York Times*, June 29, 2018

WHAT CAN WE do to stand up to racism? We can start with conversations: talking to our children and grandchildren about racism, to our parents and grandparents, our friends and family, our colleagues, our followers on social media. We can read up on the history, listening to and learning from black people and their experiences. And we can check our privilege. Too many of us white people tend to be unaware of the advantages we have compared to black people....I've had access to capital, to support, to the trust of my peers. None of that would have been available to a black person with the same ambition. Yes, much has changed and improved. But not enough.

—**"Listening and learning from our partners,"** *Virgin*,
June 9, 2020

Active Virgin Companies as of 2020

- Connect Airways (Flybe)
- Virgin Active
- Virgin Balloon Flights
- Virgin Atlantic
- Virgin Australia
- Virgin Books
- Virgin Care
- Virgin Experience Days
- Virgin Galactic
- Virgin Holidays
- Virgin Hotels
- Virgin Hyperloop One
- Virgin Limited Edition
- Virgin Limobike
- Virgin Media (Liberty Global)
- Virgin Megastores
- Virgin Mobile
- Virgin Money
- Virgin Oceanic
- Virgin Orbit
- Virgin Pulse
- Virgin Racing
- Virgin Radio
- Virgin Rail
- Virgin Sports
- Virgin Trains
- Virgin Unite
- Virgin Startup
- Virgin Vacations
- Virgin Voucher
- Virgin Voyages

Retired or Sold Virgin Products and Companies

- Absolute Radio
- Air Nigeria
- Radio Free Virgin
- Student magazine
- Virgin Airship and Balloon Company
- Liquid Comics
- Vie at Home
- Virgin America
- Virgin Bikes
- Virgin Brides
- Virgin Cars
- Virgin Charter
- Virgin Cinemas
- Virgin Clothing
- Virgin Digital Help
- Virgin Drinks
- Virgin Cola
- Virgin Vodka
- v-Mix
- Virgin Electronics
- Virgin Energy

- Virgin Express
- V Festival
- V Festival
- Virgin Festival
- Virgin Films
- Virgin Games
- Virgin Green Fund
- Virgin Health Bank
- Virgin Interactive
- Virgin Limousines
- Virgin Media
- Virgin Media UK
- Virgin Mobile Australia
- Virgin Mobile Canada
- Virgin Mobile France
- Virgin Mobile India
- Virgin Mobile USA
- Virgin Money Australia
- Virgin Money US
- Virgin One account

- Virgin Spa
- Virgin Sun Airlines
- Virgin Play
- Virgin Snow
- Virgin Trains ExpressCoach
- Virgin CrossCountry
- Virgin EMI Records
- Virgin Records
- Virgin Racing
- Virgin Vodka
- Virginware
- Virgin Wines
- Virgin Trains
- Virgin Trains East Coast

Milestones

1950

- Richard Branson is born on July 18 in Blackheath, a suburb of London.

1966

- Branson drops out of school at age 16.

1968

- The first issue of *Student* magazine publishes.

1970

- Branson launches Virgin as a mail-order record business.

- The Virgin Group is founded as the umbrella company to all future Virgin businesses.

1971

- The first Virgin record store opens.

- Branson spends a night in prison for tax evasion. He is convicted of avoiding customs and excise taxes on the records he is selling.

1972

- Virgin opens a recording studio called The Manor.
- Branson marries Kristen Tomassi.

1973

- Virgin Records and Virgin Music Publishing launch. The first album released is *Tubular Bells,* by Mike Oldfield. The album is a commercial success.
- The first track of *Tubular Bells* is used as the theme for the 1973 film *The Exorcist.*

1978

- Branson purchases the uninhabited Necker Island, part of the British Virgin Islands.

1979

- The first Virgin Megastore opens.
- Branson and Tomassi divorce.

1984

- Virgin Atlantic launches with a flight from Gatwick to Newark.

1985

- Branson attempts the fastest Atlantic Ocean crossing, but the boat capsizes, leading to international media attention.

1986

- Virgin Group raises £30 million (about $56 million)
by going public.

1988

- Branson buys back Virgin Group and makes it private again.

1989

- Branson weds Joan Templeman at their home on Necker Island in the Caribbean. The couple's two children, Holly and Sam, are in attendance.

1990

- While crossing the Pacific Ocean in a hot-air balloon, the propane gas catches on fire. Branson and crewmate Per Lindstrand make an emergency landing on a frozen lake in Canada.

1992

- Branson sells Virgin Records to Thorn EMI for £500,000,000—about $1 billion.

1997

- Branson is named "Sexiest Businessman" by *People* Magazine.

1998

- Branson's attempt to circumnavigate the globe in a hot air balloon ends when the balloon crashes into the Pacific Ocean.

1999

- Branson is knighted for his accomplishments in entrepreneurship.

2004

- Virgin Unite, a nonprofit foundation, launches.

- Virgin Galactic, Branson's commercial space tourism company, launches. The starting price for a trip to space is roughly £130,000 (or $200,000).

2007

- Branson, Peter Gabriel, and Nelson Mandela found The Elders, a group of highly esteemed global figures who work together to solve humanitarian issues around the world. 2013 members of the group include Archbishop Desmond Tutu, former US president Jimmy Carter, and former UN Secretary-General Kofi Annan.

2009

- The last Virgin Megastores close in the US and Japan. They continue to operate in Australia for another year.

2011

- The main house of Branson's Necker Island compound burns down. Actress Kate Winslet, a guest of the family, rescues Branson's mother from the fire.

2012

- Virgin Money UK purchases Northern Rock, a British Bank.

- At the 54th Grammy Awards, Branson receives the President's Merit Award for his contributions to the music industry.

- Virgin Galactic successfully completes its 23rd test flight.

2013

- Virgin Active launches its Singapore location, the company's first club in Asia.

- Branson announces that Virgin Galactic will be ready for its first passengers by the end of the year or in the first quarter of 2014.

- Virgin Galactic's SpaceShipTwo (SS2) brakes the sound barrier at 55,000 feet during a successful rocket-powered flight.

- Branson joins Bill Gates' $500bn philanthropy club and commits to giving away half his fortune to philanthropic causes.

- The main house of Branson's Necker Island re-opens after being rebuilt for two years. It now costs $60,000 a night for visitors to rent.

2014

- Virgin Galactic receives clearance from the U.S. government to begin planning space flights.

- SpaceShipTwo (SS2) mis launches over the Mojave Desert and crashes, injuring the pilot and killing the copilot. Branson says he plans to restore public faith in Virgin Galactic and move forward with space travel.

- Branson hosts a summit to work up a plan to turn the Caribbean Islands "green" with renewable energy, which includes converting Necker and Moskito to 75-80% renewable energy.

2015

- Branson invested in a venture called OneWeb Ltd. to provide worldwide satellite-internet service.

- Branson announces Virgin Cruises, his new venture into the cruise industry, which will have three cruise ships carrying 2,860 passengers and will be based in Miami, Florida.

- Branson and group of international business leaders make a call to governments to pledge a zero-net-emission target for 2025, saying that this goal will build prosperity, grow businesses, and drive innovation.

2016

- Branson announces that Virgin America will be merging with Alaska Air.

- Virgin Galactic unveils new iteration of Space-ShipTwo, called VSS Unity, which features improved safety features.

- Branson launches pro-EU campaign to warn the public in Britain of the economic dangers of Brexit.

- Branson unveils prototype aircraft, which flies at speeds of 1,451 mph making a London to New York trip just over three hours.

2017

- Branson takes shelter in the wine cellar of his private home as Hurricane Irma hits Necker Island and destroys several buildings.

- Branson invests in Hyperloop One to develop ground transportation that moves at airline speeds from the use of magnetic levitation.

2018

- The VSS Unity breaks the sound barrier in a successful test flight, the first rocket-powered test flight since the 2014 crash of the SpaceShipTwo.

- Branson and his son are nearly killed by massive falling boulders as they climb Mont Blanc.

- Branson announces that he is acquiring the Hard Rock casino in Las Vegas.

2019

- Virgin Galactic sends first test passenger to space.

- Virgin Voyages officially opens and starts taking bookings for first cruise ship, The Scarlet Lady.

- Branson takes lead in billionaire space race, ahead of Elon Musk and Jeff Bezos.

- Branson celebrates 30 years of marriage to Joan Templeman.

2020

- Branson postpones the launch of Virgin Voyages first cruise due to threats of the coronavirus pandemic.

- Branson's rocket company Virgin Orbit beings ventilator project to embark on mass producing ventilators to help the United States fight coronavirus.

- Virgin Galactic creates prototype of oxygen hoods for patients suffering coronavirus.

Acknowledgments

Thank you to Hannah Masters for her invaluable contribution to the preparation of this manuscript.